DEDICATION

This book is dedicated to my first Grandson Kawai.

INTRO

It wasn't until I had a Grandson that I realized that so many little boys are obsessed with Trash Trucks. I think my Grandson said Trash Truck before he said Mom or Dad.
He always looks forward to the day the trash truck comes down the road. We must stop everything and acknowledge the trash truck.
So, this is for all the little boys who love Trash Trucks. I hope you will enjoy the adventure of Tom and Toby the Trash Truck as they make friends

Beep beep! Beep beep!
When his alarm went off, Tom jumped out of bed and ran to the window.

It was his favorite day of the week.
The day the trash truck came down the street!

Tom waved through the window as he watched the truck rumble toward their house.
But as he did so, something caught his eye…

Sticking out of the trashcan was his favorite toy.
His very own trash truck!
He'd been playing with it outside. Someone
must have thought it was meant for the trash.

As quick as a flash, Tom ran downstairs. He ran through the kitchen and down the hall, but when he got outside...
The trash truck had already gone!

There was only one thing for it...
FOLLOW THAT TRASH TRUCK!

CAUTION

Grabbing his scooter and his helmet, Tom raced down the street.
He followed the little trail of trash until he reached where the trash truck was headed.

The trash dump!

Tom had never seen anything like it.

There were piles of trash everywhere, full of all the things people throw out.

As Tom looked around, he heard something behind him.

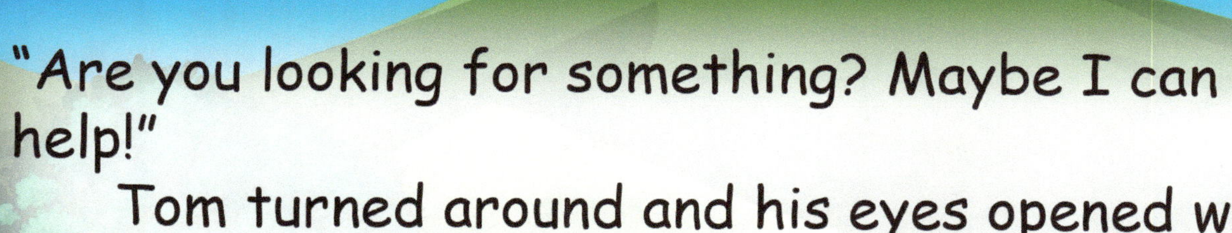

"Are you looking for something? Maybe I can help!"

Tom turned around and his eyes opened wide. It was the trash truck!

"I'm Toby," said the track truck. "Welcome to my home! This is where I bring all the trash, ready for it to be recycled."

Tom was trying to hold in his excitement. He'd always wanted to talk to the trash truck!
     But then he remembered why he had followed him all the way here.

"You took something this morning that wasn't supposed to be trash!" Tom said.
Toby looked surprised.
    "Not trash? What have you lost? I know where absolutely everything is around here."

Tom told Toby about his toy truck, and Toby's eyes lit up.

    As he turned around, Tom saw straight away where he was looking.

"Everything you see here can be used as something else. Just watch this!"

Tom watched as Toby the trash truck drove around, searching among all the piles.

At the very top of a big, wobbly pile of trash he saw it.

His trash truck!

"How am I going to reach it?" Tom said. "I can't climb up there!"

"Let me tell you a little secret..." said Toby.

"Like this!" he said, opening up his rear loader.
"You can use this broom to get up higher!"

Tom held onto the broom and leaped high into the air.

In a second, he was almost at the top of the mountain!

But his truck was still too far away.

"And this!" said Toby. "You can use these shoelaces like a rope!"
HONK

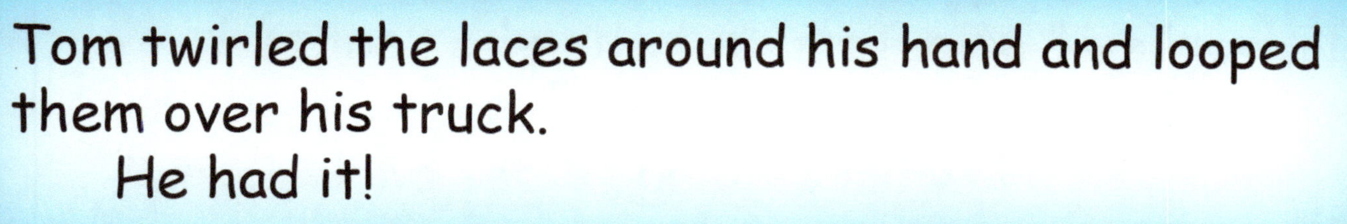

Tom twirled the laces around his hand and looped them over his truck.
He had it!

"It worked!" said Tom. But then he realized something...
"How am I going to get back down?"

As he opened his loader, Tom saw something fly toward him.

A big picnic blanket!

Toby honked his horn and zoomed all around,
looking at every piece of trash there was.
"Aha!" he said. "I've found it!"

"This could be a parachute!" they both said together.

Holding up the blanket, Tom floated through the air, with his truck safely under his arm.

Toby opened his door and Tom landed on the front seat, bouncing up and down.
"That was amazing!" he said.

"Everything here can be used as something else!" said Toby the trash truck, smiling wide. "If you ever need me, just HONK!"

Tom waved goodbye as Toby drove down the street.

With his truck under his arm, Tom knew he'd never look at trash the same way again.